Jayce's ALPHABET RULES

A

B

C

BY JAYCE JOYCE

Copyright ©2024 by Jayce Joyce
ISBN : 978-1-7393027-2-6

Published in the United Kingdom in March 2024 by Jayce's World
Illustrated by Paul Oke
Designed by @nwado

All rights reserved. No part of this book may be reproduced or transmitted in any form or by any means, electronic or mechanical, including photocopying, recording, or by an information storage and retrieval system - except by a reviewer who may quote brief passages in a review to be printed in a magazine or newspaper - without permission in writing from the copyright owner.

CONTENT

Amusement Park Rules —————————————— 4
Brushing Teeth Rules —————————————— 6
Classroom Rules ———————————————— 8
Dentist Rules ————————————————— 10
Exercise Rules ————————————————— 12
Fire Alarm Rules ————————————————— 14
Garden Rules —————————————————— 16
Hospital Rules —————————————————— 18
Ice Skating Rules ————————————————— 20
Jigsaw Puzzle Rules ———————————————— 22
King Visit Rules —————————————————— 24
Library Rules ——————————————————— 26
Mealtime Rules —————————————————— 28
Nature Walk Rules (Forest School) ——————————— 30
Outdoor Playground Rules ———————————————— 32
Picnic Rules ———————————————————— 34
Quiz Rules ———————————————————— 36
Road Traffic Rules ————————————————— 38
Supermarket Rules ————————————————— 40
Toilet Rules ——————————————————— 42
Unicorn Rules ——————————————————— 44
Vacation Rules —————————————————— 46
Washing Hand Rules ————————————————— 48
X Marks The Spot Rules ———————————————— 50
Yo-yo Craft Rules ————————————————— 52
Zoo Rules ———————————————————— 54
Author's Biography ————————————————— 56

Ready to have some fun?

A AMUSEMENT PARK RULES

1. Get ready!
2. Go to the theme park.
3. Go on the rides.
4. Let others have a go.
5. Go on other rides.
6. Have a drink.
7. Go on more rides.
8. Go home feeling happy.
9. Have a bath and some rest.
10. Dream about what you will do on your next adventure.

Do you want to smile for the world?

B BRUSHING TEETH RULES

1. Get ready!
2. Grab your toothbrush.
3. Put a pea-sized amount of toothpaste on your toothbrush.
4. Brush your teeth left, right, up and down.
5. Clench your teeth together and brush.
6. Stick your tongue out and brush.
7. Get a cup of water, rinse your mouth and spit it out.
8. Rinse your toothbrush and put away.
9. Smile for the world, hooray!
10. Do this every morning when you wake up and at night before you go to bed.

Do you want to learn and play?

C CLASSROOM RULES

1. Get ready!
2. Go to school.
3. Greet your teachers and friends.
4. Register time.
5. Assembly time.
6. Phonics time.
7. Maths time.
8. Lunchtime.
9. Playtime
10. Story time.
11. Say goodbye to your teachers and friends.

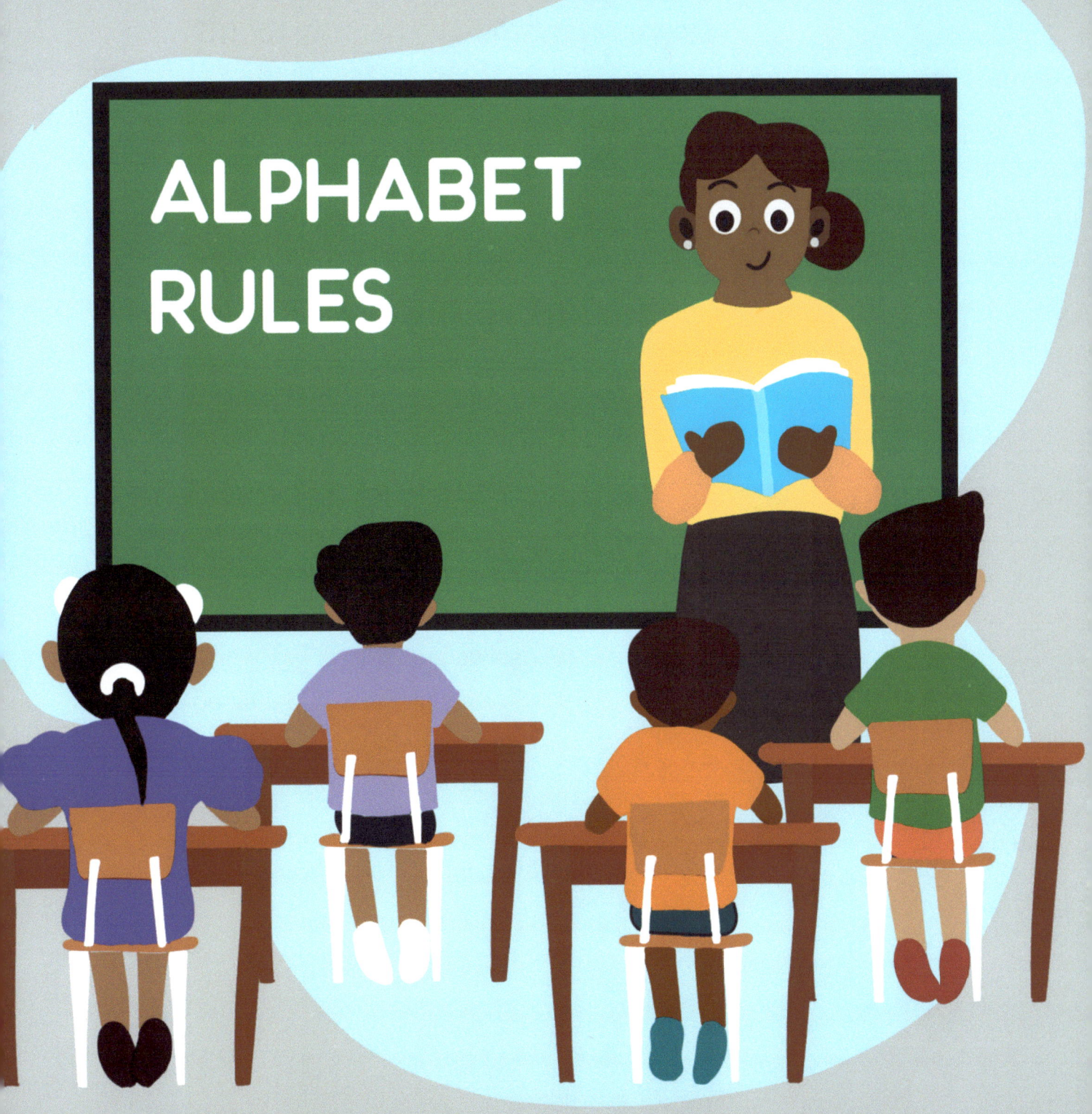

Do you want to have healthy teeth?

 **DENTIST RULES**

1. Get ready!
2. Go to the dentist.
3. The dentist checks your teeth using a dental probe.
4. The dentist checks far places in your mouth using a dental mirror.
5. The dentist uses a scaler to remove all the dirt from your teeth.
6. The dentist uses suction to remove saliva and dirt.
7. The dentist uses a dental polisher to remove plaque.
8. Smile for the world to see your clean teeth.
9. Go home feeling happy.

Do you want to stay fit?

E **EXERCISE RULES**

1. Get ready!
2. Wear comfortable clothes.
3. Wear comfortable shoes.
4. Go to the gym.
5. Warm up.
6. Stretch.
7. Take your time.
8. Drink plenty of fluid.
9. Cool down.
10. Go home feeling happy.

Do you want to stay safe?

F FIRE ALARM RULES

1. Get ready!
2. If there is a fire alarm, don't be scared, stay calm, don't yell, don't run and don't scream!
3. Follow instructions from a grown-up.
4. Get out of the building slowly and calmly.
5. Be still if a grown-up has asked you to.
6. Make sure that everyone is present and safe.
7. Do not talk needlessly.
8. When the fire alarm has stopped, follow instructions from a grown-up.
9. Go back into the building slowly.
10. Stay safe!

Do you want to do some gardening?

G GARDEN RULES

1. Get ready!
2. Go to the garden centre.
3. Get soil, planting pots and seeds.
4. Put the soil inside a planting pot.
5. Put the seed inside the pot.
6. Water the seeds so that they can grow.
7. Check your plant daily to see if it is growing nicely.
8. For fruits and vegetables, harvest once they are ready.
9. For flowers, leave them inside the pot.
10. Keep watering flowers daily.

Not feeling well, stomach ache, cold, cough, sore throat, flu?

H   HOSPITAL RULES

1. Get ready!
2. Go to the doctor.
3. The doctor checks your mouth using an endoscope.
4. The doctor checks your ears with an otoscope.
5. The doctor uses his/her hands to check your stomach.
6. The doctor checks your heartbeat with a stethoscope.
7. The doctor checks your temperature with a thermometer.
8. The doctor checks your pulse with a pulse machine.
9. The Doctor checks your blood pressure with a blood pressure machine.
10. The doctor prescribes medicine if needed.
11. Go back home feeling better.

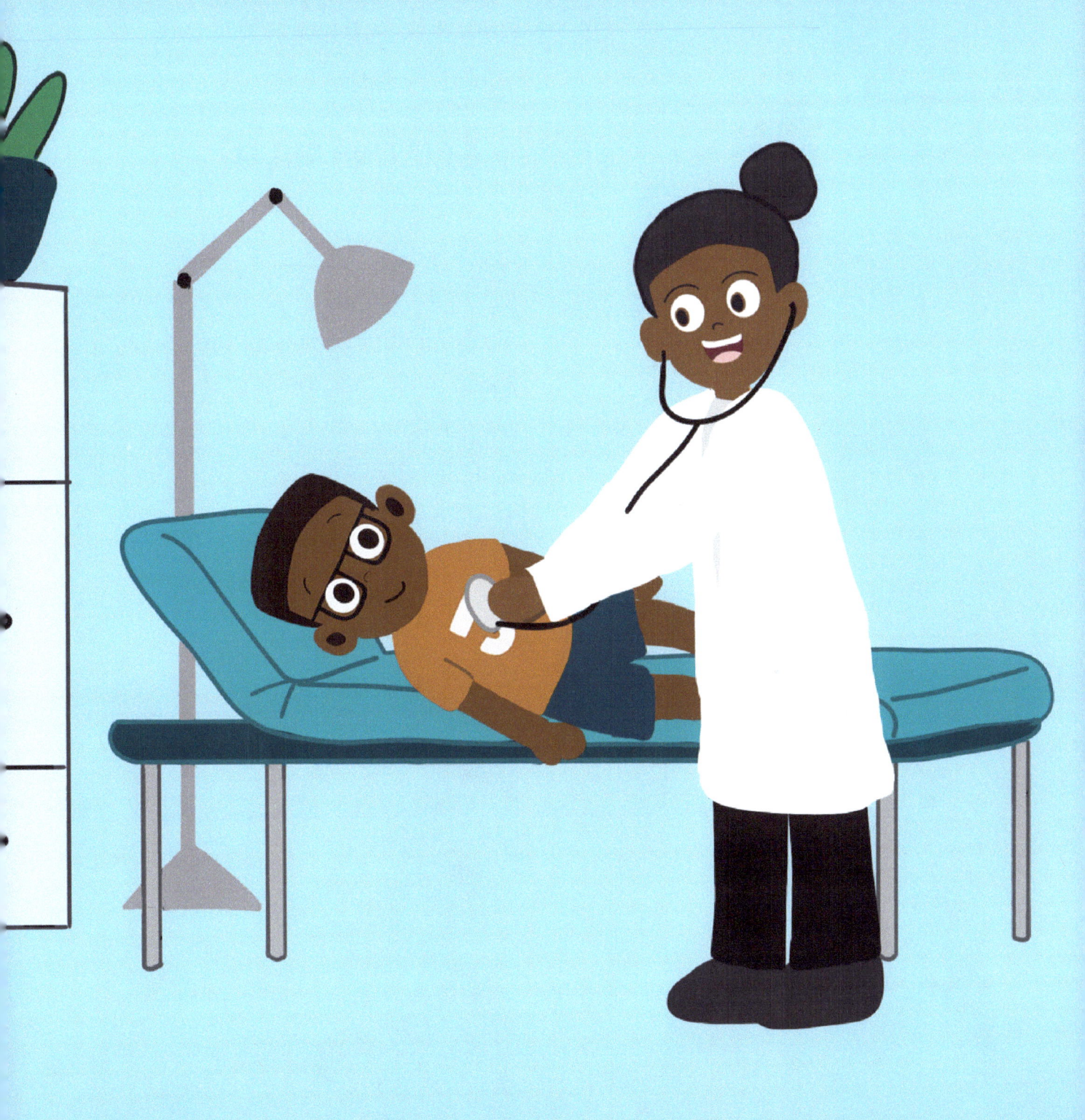

Do you want to ice skate?

1 ICE SKATING RULES

1. Get ready!
2. Go to the skating rink.
3. Follow instructions from the staff.
4. Keep moving all the time.
5. Do not carry others while skating.
6. Drink plenty of fluid.
7. Cool down.
8. Go home feeling happy.

Do you want to have fun and learn?

JIGSAW PUZZLE RULES

1. Get ready!
2. Have a good look at the puzzle picture.
3. Take puzzle pieces out of the box.
4. Sort out puzzle pieces into different shapes and sizes.
5. Look for pictures with similar colours.
6. Find the corners and place them correctly.
7. Build the outside.
8. Build the inside.
9. Match them correctly.
10. Enjoy your hard work.

Do you want to visit the King?

KING VISIT RULES

1. Get ready!
2. Go to the clothing shop.
3. Buy an extremely smart outfit.
4. Get dressed.
5. Go to Buckingham Palace.
6. Greet the guards.
7. Meet the KING!
8. Bow if you are a boy.
9. Curtsy if you are a girl.
10. Tell the king all the good things you do to look after the environment.
11. Say goodbye.

Colour me in!

BUCKINGHAM PALACE

Do you want to read a book?

L LIBRARY RULES

1. Get ready!
2. Go to the library.
3. Get some books.
4. Read the books/borrow.
5. Go to the screen.
6. Follow instructions and borrow.
7. Put books in your bag.
8. Go home and read.
9. Return books on time so that others can borrow and read too.
10. Happy reading!

Are you hungry?

MEALTIME RULES

1. Get ready!
2. Set the table with cutleries.
3. Have food on the table.
4. Eat food and drink water. It helps to digest your food.
5. Put all the cutleries away.
6. Clean up the table.
7. Wash all cutleries.
8. Put them away.
9. You are done.

Feeling able to enjoy nature?

NATURE WALK RULES

1. Get ready!
2. Go to a nature park/forest.
3. Explore nature.
4. Look out for signs and notices around.
5. Think about the plants and animals in the place.
6. Be friendly to them and treat them nicely.
7. Do not damage, leave no litter.
8. Watch, listen and ask questions.
9. Only touch safe animals and plants.
10. Go home feeling happy.

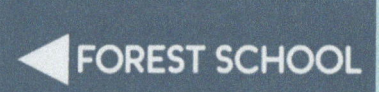

Colour me in!

Colour me in!

Feeling like having fun?

0 OUTDOOR PLAYGROUND RULES

1. Get ready!
2. Wear the appropriate clothing.
3. Go to the playground.
4. Explore all the equipment.
5. Do not play on wet equipment.
6. Ask questions.
7. Play with your friends if any.
8. Play nicely together.
9. Have a drink.
10. Go home feeling happy.

Do you want to have fun, explore and learn?

P PICNIC RULES

1. Get ready!
2. Get sandwiches, fruits, vegetables, and drinks.
3. Go to your picnic destination.
4. Look around, play games, sing songs, learn and discover nature.
5. Have snacks.
6. Explore things that you have not seen before.
7. Thank the staff if any.
8. Go home feeling happy.

Colour me in!

Do you want to study better and be smart?

QUIZ RULES

1. Get ready!
2. Listen to your teacher in school.
3. Work with your classmates in small groups.
4. Study at home.
5. Study the type of quiz you are taking.
6. Give plenty of time when studying.
7. Be happy when studying.
8. Take your quiz with confidence.
9. Praise yourself for your hardwork.
10. Treat yourself.

What is the time on the clock?

Colour me in!

Do you want to keep safe on the roads?

 **ROAD TRAFFIC RULES**

1. Get ready!
2. Know your signals.
3. Stop, look left, look right and cross if it is safe to do so.
4. Always listen for cars before crossing.
5. Do not run on the road.
6. Always use sidewalks.
7. Do not stick your hands or head outside a moving car.
8. Do not crossroad at bending corners.
9. Slow down when approaching speed bumps.
10. Do not rush when getting out of the car

Do you want to stay healthy

SUPERMARKET RULES

1. Get ready!
2. Go to the supermarket.
3. Get a cart.
4. Sanitise the cart.
5. Shop for healthy foods.
6. Go to the checkout.
7. Follow the queue and don't push in.
8. Use self-checkout if available.
9. Sanitise your hands.
10. Exit the supermarket.

Feeling like going to the toilet?

T TOILET RULES

1. Get ready!
2. Go to the toilet.
3. Do a wee or poo.
4. Clean your bottom using toilet tissue.
5. Flush the toilet.
6. Wash hands with soap and warm water.
7. Dry hands using a hand towel or paper towel.
8. Close the toilet and leave.
9. You are done.

Do you want to have some fun?

U UNICORN RULES

1. Get ready!
2. Minimum of 2-8 players needed.
3. Shuffle the deck.
4. Give each player 5 cards from the black deck.
5. Each player chooses one baby unicorn card from the white deck.
6. Each time you start your turn, pick up one card from the black deck.
7. Play a unicorn card from your hand.
8. Play a magic card from your hand.
9. Draw another card from the deck.
10. The first person to collect 7 unicorns in their stable wins.

Do you want to have a fun vacation?

VACATION RULES

1. Get ready!
2. Have breakfast.
3. Do 15 minutes of reading.
4. Do 15 minutes of writing, drawing or colouring.
5. Clean up one room at home.
6. Play around for 30 minutes.
7. Do 15 minutes of maths.
8. Make or build something using your wide imagination.
9. Help your family, a neighbour or a friend.
10. Watch electronics for 30 minutes ONLY!

Colour me in!

Are your hands dirty?

 WASHING HAND RULES

1. Get ready!
2. Wet hands with warm water.
3. Put soap and scrub.
4. Make lather.
5. Scrub your wrists, between your fingers, and under your nails.
6. Rinse hands very well.
7. Dry hands using a hand towel, paper towel, or hand dryer.
8. Put the used paper towel in the bin.
9. All the germs are gone.

Do you want to have fun finding Pirate Gold?

X MARKS THE SPOT RULES

1. Get ready!
2. Bury treasure in the sand.
3. Everyone should guess where the treasure is hiding.
4. Mark the spots as they guess.
5. Dig where you put your X Marks the Spot.
6. Whoever finds the treasure WINS!
7. Collect your spot markers.
8. The winner reburies the treasure for the next round.

Do you want to make your own yo-yo?

Y YO-YO CRAFT RULES

1. Get a pair of bottle caps.
2. Join the caps with a small screw.
3. Tie the yo-yo onto a string.
4. Add any character of your choice with beautiful decorations.
5. Throw the yo-yo, making sure it is attached to the string.
6. Hold the string tight to your finger.
7. You are done.

Colour me in!

Do you want to learn and have fun?

Z   ZOO RULES

1. Get ready!
2. Get a map or guidebook at the reception.
3. Plan a route around the zoo.
4. Drive/walk around the zoo.
5. Explore all the different animals.
6. Do not feed the animals, they can become ill.
7. Do not make loud noises or try to scare the animals.
8. Follow directions from the zookeeper.
9. If there is a talk, ask questions at the end.
10. Wait for your turn if you want to see an animal.
11. Go home feeling happy!

AUTHOR'S BIOGRAPHY

Jayce's five golden rules for every child to develop their creative writing skills are: "Think it, say it, love it, write it, and inspire."

Jayce Joyce is a highly gifted five-year-old British author from Birmingham, United Kingdom. He earned a World Record title as the youngest author to publish a book series simultaneously at the age of four, following the publication of his first book series titled "Jayce's Sweet Tooth" and "A Beach With No Sea". He is currently one of the youngest members of Mensa and Potential Plus UK.

Jayce's passion for reading and writing started as early as 15 months when he would try to understand pictures in storybooks and attempt to draw them on a board with an excellent tripod grip. By the age of three, Jayce could read and write an entire script of whatever he had seen or heard. He would always return home from nursery with scripts he had written or illustrated for the day. By the time Jayce was about to leave nursery, he was encouraged by his teachers to start exploring story structure and begin writing his own stories.

He loves to play with language, incorporating silly rhymes and funny alliterations into his writing. He draws on family experiences and world knowledge to inspire his imaginative writing.

www.ingramcontent.com/pod-product-compliance
Lightning Source LLC
Chambersburg PA
CBHW041520070526
44585CB00002B/23